Eagles Were Made To Fly

INSPIRATIONAL POEMS BY PASTOR, EARL J. BAKER, JR

ISBN 978-1-63844-352-0 (paperback)
ISBN 978-1-63844-353-7 (digital)

Christian Faith Publishing
832 Park Avenue
Meadville, PA 16335
www.christianfaithpublishing.com

Printed in the United States of America

Eagles Were Made To Fly

It wasn't long ago that God sovereignly saw,
That my sister and I had a ma and a pa.
It was there in the nest, we were placed so high;
For eagles were made to fly.

From that well built home that's called a nest,
We were cared for daily, and encouraged to rest.
Each day we were nurtured by ma and pa.
They brought meat to eat from near and far.

Our wings grew long and our bodies grew stronger.
Our legs grew straight, and our feathers grew longer.
We were so happy in our home on high,
Ma and pa and my sister and I.

Now ma and pa began to act strange.
In fact sis and I thought that they were deranged.
They began to move parts of the nest away.
It wasn't quite clear what they were trying to say.

For sis and I were not very old.
They were trying to tell us what had not been told.
We became kind of sleepy like we did at night.
Then ma and pa said, we must take our first flight.

To be perfectly honest, it didn't seem fair,
But eagles were made to go to the air.
Ma and pa knew what was best,
So they gently shoved and we fell out of the nest.
At first it was frightful; I thought I would die.
But eagles were made to fly.

We tumbled and tumbled from our home on high,
Then we moved our wings, and we started to fly.
It was awful at first, we were feeling quite poor,
Then it wasn't long, we were learning to soar.

*****

Now the moral of the story that you have just heard.
Is that you and I are much like that bird.
We weren't made to be lazy, and doze in the nest
We were made to be stirred from our earthly rest.

We were made to set our sights much higher.
We were created to be a heavenly flyer.
We were made to please God, rather than man,
As we set our sights on that heavenly land.

Unto Christ we must live, and to self we must die.
For we like the eagle were made to fly.

Written by Pastor. Earl J. Baker. Jr.

Scripture: Colossians 3:1-2; Ephesians 2:6

"If ye then be risen with Christ, seek those things which are above,
where Christ sitteth on the right hand of God.
Set your affection on things above, not on things on the earth".

"And hath raised us up together, and made us sit together in heavenly
places in Christ Jesus".

4

If I Had But One Wish

He said, if I had but one wish, I'd like to have a million dollars.
I heard another say, if I had but one wish, I'd
like to move up with the scholars.

I went to the school yard and heard the children say,
If I had but one wish, I'd like to play all day.

If I had but one wish, said the drunkard, I would like a bigger glass.
Then I heard the harlot wish, if the night would only last.

I heard a godly mother say, if I had but one wish,
I'd wish my children to walk with God, and never a day to miss.

I heard the down-and-outer say, if I had but one wish,
I'd like to have some clothes to wear, and
some food to put in my dish.

Then I listened to the farmer as he made his wish so plain.
I only wish for a greater harvest, from the seed and planted grain.

I visited the hospital and I heard the afflicted complain,
If I had but one wish, it would be to ease this pain.

I walked to the edge of the woods one day,
and there stood a lonely man
He said, if I had but one wish, it would
be for a friend to take my hand.

I then saw a man with a thorn pierced brow,
and much love upon his face,
Lifting his nail scared hands toward heaven,
with tenderness and grace.
He said, if I had but one wish, it would surely be,
To redeem all the people of earth, from eternal calamity.

Written by Pastor, Earl J. Baker, Jr.

How Sweet It Is

How sweet it is when all is well with thy soul,
Are you're still rejoicing as in days of old.
Your heart is free and your head is clear,
You're a child of God with nothing to fear.

How sweet it is when the blossoms bear,
With a sweet smelling fragrance all through the air
It is hard to believe that Spring has come,
Winter has passed and the cold winds gone.

How sweet it is to be with a friend,
One you can trust to the very end;
One you can like and one you can love'
It's that special one who is sent from above.

How sweet it is when a baby cries.
It is sweeter yet when a Christian dies.
Death is made sweeter it seems to be,
When a soul is prepared for eternity.

How sweet it is to have faith in God,
As you travel each day on this earthly sod.
Just to reach out and touch his unseen hand,
While pressing onward to that promised land.

How sweet it is to receive a gift.
It comes at a time when you need a lift.
It may not be much, just a token of love,
In reality my friend, it comes from above.

How sweet it is to have a Father so kind;
One who keeps us ever on his mind.
He knows and cares for the sparrow that falls,
And listens intently to each child who calls

How sweet it is to have health and strength,
Bread on the table and water to drink;
A few clothes to wear, and a place to abide,
As each day passes, just trusting in God.

How sweet it to have a good job,
A name and God's favor, that no man can rob.
These are only some thoughts, and it's plain to see,
That God really cares for you and me.

Written By Pastor, Earl J. Baker Jr.

I Am Acquainted With His Power

When I am lonely Christ is my dearest friend
He promised to be with me, even to the end.

When I am torn by the adversary he's always by my side,
The one who is there to defend me, is my Lord, the crucified.

Once I picked up the sword to defend myself.
He quickly moved in to protect me, with quietness and stealth.

There are times when fear attacks me, and there is no place to hide.
Then my loving Shepherd, presses me closer to his side.

On days when sin overwhelms me, and
temptation surrounds me sore,
He offers a place of sweet refuge, and directs me to eternity's shore.

Oft-times the adversary approaches from
behind, as Pharaoh at Israel's Red Sea,
And the dear Lord softly whispers, stand
still, and I will open for thee.

Satan tempts me to return to Egypt land,
with pleasure abounding for me,
Then the Captain of my salvation, steps in to keep me free.

When I come to the water of Marah, though bitter as it may be,
He lifts the cup from his fountain, and says,
drink, I have saved it for thee.

As Joshua, I have fought with Amalek, and
it seemed that he would prevail,
But Jehovah sent Aaron and Hur to help me,
with my hands lifted I could not fail.

Oft-times my hands were so heavy, I felt I was standing alone,
Then strangely enough, beneath me, God placed his heavenly stone.

While in the desert of wandering, with serpents all around,
I felt that I was dying, and then did grace abound.

I cried out, Lord, I've been bitten, and now I can hardly see,
Then he said, my child it's not over, just look to Calvary.

By Pastor, Earl J. Baker, Jr.

An Endless Day

The closer I come to the end of the way,
The more I desire that endless day.

Earth's hopes and dreams all fade away,
In view O the coming endless day.

An endless day; all sorrow and trouble disappear.
Earth's life will be done without reason to fear.

Here and now, sweat and toil to stay,
But oh, for the thoughts of an endless day.

There's sickness and pain in the land of now,
Soon twill come to an end, when at Christ feet we bow.

Oh, what a Saviour, who for my sins did pay,
Oh, what provision, for that endless day.

There isn't much here for hope to cling to,
Rather reason for dismay,
With loneliness and dread of the future,
Apart from an endless day.

Written by Pastor, Earl J. Baker, Jr.

Scripture: John 14:1-3; 3:16

"Let not your heart be troubled: ye believe
in God, believe also in me.
In my Father's house are many mansions: if it were not so I would
Have told you, and if I go and prepare a place for you, I will come
Again and receive you unto myself; that
where I am, there ye may be also."
For God so loved the world, that he gave his
only begotten Son, that whosoever
Believeth in him should not parish, but have everlasting life."

The Story Told That Was Never Heard

Never a moment has passed that I didn't think,
That some day I would be able to eat and drink.
The thought of coming out of darkness into light,
Was my fondest hope and greatest delight.
Since the day of my conception I have wanted to see,
My brothers and sisters and family.
I had always been comfortable and very content,
A message from God that was soon to be sent.
I had hoped that my entrance into the world,
Would be somewhat glorious as a flag unfurled.

Then something happened that I can't explain,
Until that moment, I had felt no pain.
It suddenly happened without any warning,
Then I knew that I would never see morning.
The pain was so excruciating that I could hardly bear,
I knew in a moment that it wasn't a night-mare.
I thought they loved me through and through,
But I soon realized that that wasn't true.
They didn't want me, I would be an intrusion.
So they poisoned me with a saline solution.
My skin burned and my lungs were filled,
Just another story of a baby that was killed.
A horror story told in the night,
Because the supreme court gave women the right.

What does God think of this kind of behavior?
And what if they had done this to our wonderful Savior.
Does God really care that folks act this way?
They will certainly find out on judgment day.
Men usually do as they will,
But God's word hath said, "Thou shalt not kill".

Written by Pastor Earl J Baker, Jr.
1/6/2006

Soul Searching

As I knelt one day, I began to pray,
My thoughts were cluttered and went astray.

I said, Dear Lord, you know my heart,
Help me to think; then I thought.

I'm not the man that I ought to be,
My self-life has kindled no love for thee.

Please lift my slothful soul away,
From the things that cause me to go astray.

As I prayed to God my heart was lifted
My thoughts were gathered and everything shifted

I began to express my sorrow to him,
For my life had been painfully shameful and grim.

I told him of my need for his strength in my life,
I prayed for my children and my lovely wife.

I asked for concern for the souls of men,
And not be careless as I had been.

My love for his word had dampened a bit,
As I knew right away that this was it.

The Spirit of the Lord spoke to my heart,
As he said, My child, you need a fresh start.

So he spoke to me of my need to pray,
And get in God's word day after day.

My need to tell others of God's saving love,
And his promise to us of his mansions above.

I must endure the hardships of life,
Persecutions and sufferings that cut like a knife.

I must be true and honest to all,
And discard those things that cause me to fall.

My faith in God must increase,
As I claim his promises that bring sweet peace.

By Pastor Earl J Baker, Jr.
February 1997

God Shut The Door

As it was in the days of Noah,
As it is today, so it was before.
The day when God shut the door.
They were eating and drinking,
And knew not their fate,
Until God shut the door,
Then they knew it was to late.

You must come today,
While the door is open wide.
It was for you dear friend,
That Christ was crucified.
It was your sins and mine,
That nailed him to the tree.
Receive him today and be saved eternally.
If you fail to trust him,
And reject him ever more,
His patience will wear thin,
And God will shut the door.

By Earl J. Baker, Jr.

The legend Of The Oak Tree

I was not hatched and I was not born.
I came from an oak tree, I'm an acorn.
One chilly day late in October I fell from a limb to the ground
I feared as I lay there, that I may never be found,
But the rains, the sun and the fertile soil,
Soon produced energy without any toil.
The place to which I had fallen was just a rut,
But soon it was evident that I was more than a nut.
After many months and years it was clear to me,
That I was here by design for all to see.
As my roots reached downward and my trunk grew tall,
My reason for being, was evident to all.
The day would come when I no longer would be,
As I had always been, just an oak tree.
I had not been left long in the forest to grow,
I had bore no fruit, I had little to show.
Two men with an ax came to carry me away,
To a place where a crowd had gathered that day.
There in the midst of those angry ones,
Was a man on whose head was a crown of thorns.
Blood was pouring in every direction.
No one seemed to care nor have any affection.
I was still uncertain why I was brought there,
To watch a man being treated so unfair.
Everyone seemed to hate him and spit in his face.
They tore off his clothes as he stood in disgrace.
The men who had taken me out of the woods,
Stood and watched as long as they could.
They suddenly shoved this poor man to the ground,
With little concern, at a scene so profound.
Then they drew forward to complete their job,
As I listened to the cursing of the angry mob.

18

After beating and mocking him they nailed him to me.
He never spoke a word nor tried to get free.
Then he spoke words so kind and so true.
He said, Father forgive them, they know not what they do.
It soon became clear why I was chosen of all,
The trees in the forest with a special call.
I count it a privilege to have been the tree,
On which they crucified my creator at Calvary.

By Pastor, Earl J. Baker Jr.
Feb. 27, 1997

Scripture: John 3:16

"For God so loved the world, that he gave his only begotten Son,
That whosoever believeth in him should not perish, but
Have everlasting life."

Always Give Thanks

When things are going well, 'tis easy to give thanks,
With food on the table and money in the bank,

When the children aren't complaining, and the car is running well.
When we're assured of our salvation and escape from a burning hell.

It's easy to give thanks for others, when others are fond of us.
But can we really say we're thankful, for that dirty unfriendly old
cuss?

It's easy to be thankful when the checks are coming in,
But are we also thankful, when they're getting kind of thin?

We're thankful for the sunshine, and thankful for the rain,
But is that thanks still present, when we're lying there in pain?

Thanks be unto God we say, when we're on top of things,
But thanks just seem to leave us, when
trouble and heart-ache clings.

We appreciate the water, when the well has not gone dry,
But is that same appreciation there, with no rain clouds in the sky?

By Earl J. Baker, Jr.

Have You Noticed?

Have you noticed,
That the grass is now greener and the sky is more blue?
It is looking like Springtime and you're ageing too.

Have you noticed,
The children getting taller and their clothes getting tight?
They're not babies anymore; you don't tuck them in at night.

Have you noticed,
The wrinkles in mom's and dad's face?
The time is now nearing, when they'll finish their race.

Have you noticed,
How each day quickly passes?
Your hair is turning gray and you're now wearing glasses.

Have you noticed,
The slowness in your pace as you walk,
How you reminisce the past as with others you talk?

Have you noticed,
These are a few things to mention,
They're reminders I'd say, so we must pay attention.

Have you noticed,
That God has numbered our days,
And God's word doth remind us to take heed to our ways.

Have you noticed,
The coming judgment for all,
for the rich and poor, the great and the small,
When each one shall stand and give an account,
for what they have done, whatever the amount?

Written by Pastor, Earl J. Baker, Jr.
1990

Scripture: Romans 14:12

"So then everyone shall give account of himself to God"

That Celestial City

Abraham looked for a city, whose builder and maker is God,
But he found it not on this earthly sod.
The reason for that is plain to see.
It was a city described as yet to be.

In Revelation chapter twenty-one we are given a scene,
Of a beautiful city all garnished and clean.
In this same chapter John tells what is told,
Of it's Jasper walls and it's street of pure gold.

It's a place so exciting, no, never a bore,
For the former things won't be any more.
Such things as death, sickness, sorrow and pain,
These are never known in that fair land.

On it's distant shore there is never a worry,
And the redeemed ones never get in a hurry.
As was told by some, 'tis the living way,
For there's no night there, 'tis always day.

In that celestial city soon to abide,
Will be the Lamb and his wife, the beautiful bride.
The bride for which he was crucified,
There he and she will always reside.

Hallelujah for the Lamb who sits on the throne,
From which flows the crystal sea.
'Tis the river of life that flows over there,
Yes, 'tis life for you and me.

But isn't it sad and isn't it a pity,
That everyone won't enter that celestial city.
It is only a place for the blessed few,
Who've been washed in the blood and created new.

Written by Pastor, Earl J. Baker, Jr.

Scripture: Rev. 21:2

"And I John saw the holy city, new Jerusalem,
coming down from God
Out of heaven, prepared as a bride adorned for her husband."

Danger Zone

One day while I was walking all alone,
I noticed a sign that said, "Danger Zone".
As I continued to walk it was plain to see.
I said, now that's just human stupidity.
It occurred to me that most folks can't read,
For they passed the sign and gave it no heed.

God's word is a sign that's plain to tell.
It warns us to flee from a place called hell.
It's a place of suffering, sorrow and pain,
A place of torment and nothing to gain.
The warning is there for those who are prone,
To walk right on past God's "Danger Zone".

Written by Pastor, Earl J. Baker, Jr.
11/24/1990

Scripture: Revelation 20:15; 21:8

"And whosoever was not found written in the book of life
was cast into the lake of fire".
"But the fearful, and unbelieving, and the
abominable, and murderers,
and whoremongers, and sorcerers, and idolaters, and all liars, shall
have their part in the lake which burneth with
fire and brimstone: which is the
second death".

The Rich Man And Lazarus

In Luke Chapter sixteen, a story is told,
Of two men, one rich and one poor.
The rich man was clothed in purple,
The poor man's clothing was sores.

The beggar man's name was Lazarus,
The rich man's name was not given.
The rich man went to hell,
And Lazarus was carried to heaven.

In hell the rich man cried for water,
To cool his burning tongue.
On earth he offered no mercy,
Neither for the old nor the young.

In hell he cried for Lazarus,
To warn his five brothers to repent
Lest they as he would enter in,
To that awful place of torment.

But Abraham said, my son, it is no need,
For if they hear not Moses and the prophets,
They'll not hear one who is risen from the dead.

This story is true as was told by our Lord,
And it serves to warn us well.
Lest we fail to trust Jesus as Saviour,
And die and be tormented in hell.

Written by Pastor, Earl J. Baker, Jr.

Concerning Faith

According to James, the apostle of God,
We should count it all joy. When our faith has been tried.
In the word of God by Peter we're told,
That the trial of our faith, is more precious than gold.
Faith is the substance of things hoped to be.
It is the evidence of things we cannot see…

Now look in Hebrews, chapter eleven.
There you'll find a list of the heroes of heaven.
In Hebrews we're told and many have heard.
That they all got to heaven by trusting God's word.

It takes faith to believe that God made the stars,
The Milky Way, Jupiter, Saturn, and Mars.
Some people say there is no solution.
But I just can't believe in this ape evolution.
Man was formed from the dust of the earth.
And from that one man came each single birth.

It was faith that caused Abel to offer blood unto God,
Instead of Cain's offering that came from the sod.
Cain offered to God the works of the flesh.
But Abel's offering pictured God's righteousness.

By faith Enoch walked with God each day,
Then God decided to take him away.
If we walk as Enoch walked, the scripture is clear,
That we too shall be caught up into the air.
Enoch's faith pleased God, as the scripture hath said,
And without it my friend, it is hell instead.

Noah was warned by God, of things to come,
So by faith he built an ark to save his home.
To the preaching of Noah, the world ignored,
But when judgment came, he was safe on board.
The ark is a type of Christ our Lord.
To be saved for eternity, just get on board.

By faith Abraham left his home,
To be led by God, to a place unknown.
As a stranger in the land, onward he went,
Looking for a city and pitching his tent.
To receive God's promise, he had to obey,
As with you and me, we shall see some day.

Sarah too, thought she was quite old,
Believed the story that God had told.
That she would give birth to a little guy,
Whose seed would be numerous as the stars in the sky.
This angelic promise came true one morn.
And Sarah gave birth, and Isaac was born.

Then Abraham's faith was tested a while,
When he was told by God to offer up this child.
Abraham believed, for God had said,
That Isaac would be blessed as the promised seed.
Abraham knew and so did his wife,
That God was able to raise him to life.

Jacob two, had great faith in God.
He both blessed and worshipped before he died.
He had faith to the end of his earthly path,
For Jacob died leaning, on the top of his staff.

Let's mention Joseph, just before he died,
Who gave commandment to Israel, where his bones would abide.
He had departing faith, in a day so grand,
When the Israelites would enter canaan land.

Then there's little Moses who was hid in the river,
By his parents, who believed in God to deliver.
By faith Moses chose to suffer with the children of God,
And lead Israel through the sea dry shod.

Then there's the faith of Joshua at Jericho town,
When they marched and shouted and the walls fell down.

Don't forget the faith of Rahab, who was saved by a scarlet cord.
When the spies came she hid them, and trusted in the Lord.
Though Rahab was a harlot she did the righteous thing,
By taking in the men of God and hanging out the string.
The wicked men of Jericho never would repent,
But Rahab's family lived, when she hid the men God sent.

Many others were mentioned in the word of God,
Who suffered great trials of affliction.
They were mocked, imprisoned and burned at the stakes,
That they might obtain a better resurrection.
Many hid themselves in dens and caves.
While others were slain by the sword.
But they all possessed one thing in common,
They truly had faith in god's word.

Written by Pastor, Earl J. Baker, Jr.

Sombody's Knocking

(By Pastor, Earl J. Baker, Jr.)

One day while I was playing,
I heard a knocking at the door.
It was just a gentle knocking,
Something I'd heard at times before.
Since I was quite young, and only a little boy,
I thought I would ignore it, I kept playing with my toy.
As years grew on the knocking seemed much louder.
Sometimes I even feared. But like most people my age,
I hadn't really cared.
My heart was very lonely and I wanted to let him in,
But Satan had his hold on me,
To continue in my sin.
Sometimes the thought occurred to me,
To go to the church and pray,
Then the great deceiver would whisper,
Not today.

Now I've grown much older,
And my heart is colder too.
I'm still neglecting to open the door,
And do what I ought to do.
It doesn't take long for the years to slip by,
And before you know it He's gone.
That stranger that stood at my heart's door as a child,
Has returned to his heavenly home.

There comes a time in everyone's life,
When he hears a knocking from a heavenly visitor.
Don't just sit there as I did,
Get up and answer the door.

Scripture: Revelation 3:20

"Behold I stand at the door, and knock: if any man hear my voice,
and open the door, I will come in to him,
and sup with him, and he with me."

When Jesus Passed By

Now the story is told of a small built man,
Who couldn't see above the crowd.
He was chief man among the publicans,
And yes, he was mighty proud.

Zacchaeus was the man,
As rich as he could be.
Being kind of short, and the crowd in the way,
Jesus he could not see.
So he pushed and shoved through the crowd that day,
And climbed up in a tree.
He had heard that Jesus would pass that way,
And Jesus he wanted to see.

Zacchaeus was told by the Lord to come down,
So he made haste and came down to the ground.
Jesus wanted to visit him,
So the publican man consented.
Now the crowd just murmured and criticized,
But Zacchaeus truly repented.

The heart of Zacchaeus was not as before,
For the half he gave we are told.
He said, if I have taken from any man,
I will gladly restore him fourfold.

Zacchaeus received and Jesus gave,
For the Lord came to seek and to save.

Written by Pastor Earl J. Baker, Jr.

Scripture: Luke 19:1-10

Forgive Me Lord

Forgive me Lord for murmuring so; I really didn't mean to.
Forgive me Lord if I seem to be ungrateful
for the many things you do.

Forgive me if I grumble, or if I may complain,
It isn't the thing to do I know, when I fuss about the rain.

I know you put up with an awful lot, hearing me talk like I do.
I must admit, I lack the faith, but you've always seen me through.

I didn't mean to act that way when Aunt Sara came to visit us.
Why, I got so mad at Clara Belle, that I almost commenced to cuss.

Forgive me Lord, for failing to kneel by my bed last night.
I know it's the thing that I should do, before I put out the light.

And Lord, I forgot to pay that debt I owe,
it's already six days behind.
Help me to think more clearly, that thing just slipped my mind.

Those thoughts in my head a few days ago,
I know they didn't make you glad.
I've thought so much on those things since
then, Lord those things were really bad.

Like Eve in the garden of Eden, I coveted, I took, I did eat.
Forgive me Lord, I'm sorry, as I humbly bow at your feet.

Forgive me Lord, for not daily reading thy word.
It's important to listen when you speak, for
when you speak, you wish to be heard.

I took a chance the other day, I gambled with a deck of cards.
I've since repented of that awful deed, a lesson learned so hard.

Forgive me Lord, for not giving more, it's
more blessed to give than to receive.
The blessings I've lost by not giving, Lord,
are blessings that can't be retrieved.

Forgive me Lord, for sitting back, and letting others do all the work.
It's my duty to help and share with the load,
a duty that's not to be shirked.

Forgive me Lord, is actually what I'm trying to say.
Those deeds, those thoughts, those words of mine,
Please forgive me when I pray.

Written by Pastor, Earl J Baker, Jr.

Christ Is All I Need

I was hungry and frail with nothing to eat.
He said, come unto me, and I will give you meat.

I was cold and naked and had nothing to wear.
He said, come unto me, I have plenty to spare.

I was unlearned and ignorant and incomplete.
He said, come unto me, and sit at my feet.

I was tired and weary and lacking much zest.
He said, come unto me, and I will give you rest.

I was rejected and lonely and about to give up.
He said, come unto me, and drink from my cup.

I was toiling hard like many other folk.
He said come unto me, and put on my yoke.

I was in prison and thought it to late.
He said come unto me, outside of the gate.

I was parched and thirsty and I nearly fell.
He said, come unto me, and drink from my well.

I was fearful and weak and nearly in shock.
He said, come unto me, and fear not little flock.

I was lost and confused and going astray.
He said, come unto me, for I am the way.

With his Christ-rejecting world, full of lust and greed,
I can truly say, Christ is all I need.

Written by Pastor, Earl J. Baker, Jr.

Scripture: Matthew 11:28
"Come unto me, all ye that labor and are heavey laden,
and I will give you rest."

It's Sunday Again

Well it's Sunday morning and it's time to go to church,
And here I sit like a bird on a perch.
They tell me that I should go to church
and get some good out of life,
But I just keep on putting it off and saying, it's not me, it's my wife,
The kids keep on asking me to go, and some day maby I will
<u>Well it's Sunday again</u>, and they're ready
to go, but I just sit here still.

One day the parson came to visit, and told me a thing or two,
But I just can't seem to get up the nerve to go and claim my pew.
The church folks have been calling and wondering what is wrong,
I keep on making excuses and singing my same old song.

<u>Well it's Sunday again</u>, and another week has gone by,
I think I'll put on my meeting clothes
and see if that sermon's so dry.
It certainly can't hurt to go and sit a spell,
in fact it might do me some good.
Deep down inside I've veen wanting to go,
and I know that I really should.

<u>Well it's Sunday again</u>, and you know, it's not so bad.
My kids keep introducing me and telling folks, "That's my dad".
It feels real good since I started and all my family likes it too.
When we go down to the church house,
we fill up the whole back pew.

<u>Well it's Sunday again</u>, and you know what?,
We're sitting almost in the front.
I've been listening to those sermons, and
that parson is really quite blunt.

38

He said if I didn't trust in the Lord and repent of my ungodly deeds,
That I would come to the judgment like the wheat and the tares,
And be burned like those unwanted weeds.

<u>Well it's Sunday again</u>, and I know that he's preaching at me,
For everything that I do and the things that
I've done, he always seems to see.
Every word that he speaks is like an arrow to my
heart, and I know what I need to do.
Next time he says come, I'll do what he says,
I'll get right up out of my pew.

<u>Well it's Sunday again</u>, and the sermon came straight to my ear.
I moved from my seat and confessed my sins,
for his salvation message was clear.

<u>Well it's Sunday again</u>, and I just can't wait
to hear from the parson again.
That parson is young and kind of spiffed up,
but he makes the meaning so plain.

Written by Pastor, Earl J. Baker, Jr.
(11/24/1991)

Scripture: Hebrews 10:25

"Not forsaking the assembling of ourselves
together, as the manner of some is;
But exhorting one another; and so much the
more as ye see the day approaching."

When Jesus Passed By

Now the story is told of a small built man,
Who couldn't see above the crowd.
He was chief man among the publicans,
And, yes, he was mighty proud.

Zacchaeus was the man,
As rich as he could be.
Being kind of short, and the crowd in the way,
Jesus he could not see.
So he pushed and shoved through the crowd that day,
And climbed up in a tree.
He had heard that Jesus would pass that way,
And Jesus he wanted to see.

Zacchaeus was told by the Lord to come down,
So he made haste and came down to the ground.
Jesus wanted to visit him,
So the publican man consented.
Now the crowd just murmured and criticized,
But Zacchaeus truly repented.

The heart of Zacchaeus was not as before,
For the half he gave we are told
He said, if I have taken from any man,
I will gladly restore him fourfold.

Zacchaeus received and Jesus gave,
For the Lord came to seek and to save.

Written by Earl J. Baker, Jr.

The Love Of God
By Pastor Earl J. Baker, Jr.
1991

Thanks be unto God
For his unfailing love,
For his everlasting mercies,
And his blessings from above.

God has always loved us humans,
With the greatest of concern,
It's a fact that only few of us,
Have ever really learned.

God's love extends to all the world,
To each and every one,
He proved his love to all of us,
By offering up his Son.

God's love is pure and spotless,
And without hypocrisy,
It's the deepest love, and the finest,
It's love in the highest degree.

It is never tainted or sordid,
With earthly carnality.
His love is not a respecter,
It shows no partiality.

The love of God is immutable,
It changes not as the wind that blows,
His love is everlasting,
No boundaries it knows.

Seeing The Invisible

Out in the shadows,
Not seen by mortal eye,
Are the spirits of unjust angels,
As they hale the victory cry.

They walk about as lions,
Seeking to devour,
The weakest of souls,
And place them in their power.

They've walked this earth for eons,
Expecting soon to win,
By subtle and covert actions,
To capture the souls of men.

From that day in Eden's garden,
When Adam and Eve did fall,
They've mustered their evil forces,
To be the lords of all.

Inside the fog of confusion,
Unseen by mortal man,
Comes the hero of the ages,
The Lord Jesus, to take command.

Had God been weak and feeble,
They surely would have won,
But the battle isn't over,
Thanks to God's dear Son.

Written by Pastor, Earl J. Baker, Jr.

Scripture: Psalm 47

God's Sea Of Forgetfulness

In the bible there's the sea of Tiberias,
Known as the sea of Galilee.
That's where Jesus taught his disciples,
Of truths for you and me.
Now there's the Crystal sea up in heaven we're told,
And the Red sea where Moses and Israel waxed bold.
There's the Salt sea into which the river Jordan falls,
And the Mediterranean known as the Great sea by all.

Did you ever read in the bible,
Where God lost his memory for sure?
Well, it was down at the sea of Forgetfulness.
Where sin was remembered no more.
Now there are other seas in the bible,
Where many strange things took place'
But I like this one best of all,
Where sin gave way to grace.

God hates sin you see.
God hates sin in you and me.
But in Christ our sins are pardoned,
Because of Calvary.
So God cast our sins in the midst of the sea,
And then lost his memory.
Now you can see why I like this sea best,
'Tis called God's sea of Forgetfulness.

When you're reminded of sins of the past,
Just remember, they're down in the sea at last.
God hath said they never shall be,
I have cast them into the depths of the sea.

Written by Pastor, Earl J. Baker, Jr.

Scripture: Micah 7:18-19

"Who is a God like unto thee, that pardoned iniquity.
And passeth by the transgression of the remnant of his heritage?
He retained not his anger forever, because he delighted in mercy.
He will turn again, he will have compassion upon us: he will subdue
Our iniquities: and thou wilt cast all their
sins into the depths of the sea".

In Times Like These

In times like these, what are thy thoughts?
Are they on having a gay old time?
Or are they on things much higher and nobler.
On things that are more sublime?

In times like these, what are thy words?
Perhaps you've dishonored God's name.
In God's book 'tis written, those who speak thus.
Shall never go without blame.

In times like these, who are thy friends.
While you're travelling along life's way?
Are they kind and patient and godly ones.
Or the kind that like to stray?

In times like these what are thy works?
Are you doing anything for the Lord?
Don't you think it's time to gather with the church.
And give an ear to God's holy word?

In times like these, what are thy hopes.
I mean thy hopes for eternity?
Have you given a thought to where you will be.
I mean in eternity?

Now that you've taken time to think on these things.
What will thy future be?

Written by Pastor, Earl J. Baker, Jr.

Scripture: Galatians 6:7

"Be not deceived: God is not mocked: for whatsoever a man soweth.
That shall he also reap."

Holidays Or Holydays

In times of festivity there is usually a cause,
But seldom it's noticed with even a pause.
We rush here and there and laugh all the way,
Without recognizing that it's a holy day.

Our days are so hurried and filled with much care
That holy days are forgotten and they end in dispare.
A holiday or a holy day, no one seems to know,
Just give me some time off and some money to blow.

Sunday was a holy day in times of old.
God's sheep were seldom found outside of the fold,
But today it's so different; it's a day like the rest.
When most folks do what they like to do best.
Many people sleep late or work on the car,
While others are found in the old town bar.
Some do yard work on God's holy day,
Until tragedy strikes, then they begin to pray.

Christmas and Easter and Thanksgiving day,
Are just times of leisure and not holy days.
Some folks regard them with very little care,
Only to observe them in the old easy chair.
My, what a blessing if they only knew,
That holidays are holy days to praise, you know who.

Yes, God wants us to enjoy ourselves,
while we give him much praise,
And think on his goodness throughout the holidays.

By Pastor, Earl J. Baker, Jr.
11-2-1990

The True Meaning Of Christmas

Christmas is the time of year,
When folks don't seem to know,
That there are things more significant,
Than holy and mistletoe.

Santa Clause and reindeer,
Are only myths you see.
Trees and lights and gifts and stuff,
Are not what it's meant to be.

On that day twenty centuries ago,
A savior was born on the earth,
The hope of his coming, was to set men free,
From a depraved and sinful birth.

God meant us to be free from death, sorrow and pain,
By trusting the Christ child's holy name.
This is the true message of Christmas to all,
That men be saved from an eternal fall.

Written by Pastor, Earl J. Baker, Jr.

About the Author

Earl Baker was born in Norfolk, VA in 1938. He came to know the Lord Jesus as his personal Savior, at the age of eleven. He began to have a hunger to study the Bible and spent many hours doing so. His Pastor asked him to teach Sunday school class. Earl began going to a home for wayward teens, and taking them the message of Salvation, and lead many of them to Christ. His Pastor began asking Earl to speak for some of the other meetings in the church, because he could see God had his hand on Earl. Earl began to feel the Lord leading him to further his studies, so he and a friend while on vacation decided to stop by Shenandoah Bible College in Roanoke, VA., there Earl enrolled for the following fall semester. The Lord has used

Earl in Pastoring several churches, and in other ministries through the years: even while doing lay jobs, like driving the city transit bus in Charleston, WV. The Lord gave Earl these poems which we pray will be a blessing to many others.

CPSIA information can be obtained
at www.ICGtesting.com
Printed in the USA
BVHW090307180123
656438BV00019B/1195

9 781638 443520